The Promise of Perfection

The Promise of Perfection

Andrew Cohen

Moksha Press 1998

Moksha Press Cataloging
Cohen, Andrew, 1955 Oct. 23-
The promise of perfection / by Andrew Cohen.
p. cm.
ISBN 1-883929-21-0
1. Spiritual Life.   2. Life.   I. Title.
BL624   299.93—dc21

Contents

Foreword

I picked up the phone in my hotel room in Albany,
New York, and the voice on the other end said, "You're not
going to believe what I'm about to tell you." I paused for a
moment. I was surprised to hear her voice. "What do you
mean?" I asked. And then quietly but very steadily she
said, "Andrew Cohen just gave a talk in Boston on *desire*,
and you're not going to believe what he said."

Albany was my last overnight stop on a journey that
had begun in San Francisco and would end the next day in
Lenox, Massachusetts. I had been a student of Andrew
Cohen's for many years when six months earlier, my own

struggles with worldly temptations had resulted in my walking out on spiritual life. Now I was returning to that life, embarrassed, humbled and with a lot of explaining to do, not just to my friends but also to myself. How had I become so lost in desire that I could step off the path to Liberation? How had I gotten to the point where spiritual life, a life that had called to me with the promise of boundless freedom, had begun to seem like an unbearable limitation itself?

My story was really the oldest in the book, and hardly needs retelling. Under the weight of desire it's not that hard to lose touch with what is most important and do things that we later regret. It's an all too painful fact of human life, and one that probably most of us to one degree or another know all too well. But until my own recent experience, I did not begin to fully appreciate the incredible power of desire, the sheer magnitude and subtlety of this force that we are all, as human beings, up against. Certainly it can be no coincidence that a great many of the central myths of our species have been about our tendency, under the influence of desire, to lose our way. *Orpheus, Faust, King Midas, Salome, Camelot*—these are but a few such stories. In Homer's *Odyssey,* even Odysseus, an adventurer of great courage and strength, humbly chooses to bind himself to the mast of his own ship rather than risk falling hopelessly under the spell of the enchanting but deadly *Sirens.*

Indeed, so many of the stories of our childhood, stories meant to prepare us for the challenge of successfully navigating this life, seem to be attempts at helping us to recognize the many forms and faces of desire. At first these stories of tragic defeat or heroic triumph seem to be dramatic exaggerations. But are they really? The Buddha spoke of desire as the root of *all human suffering.* And in fact, if one looks around at the world in which we live, the face of desire and its trail of tears is everywhere. And the dignity, peace and mystery of one whose conscience is truly clear is the rarest of jewels.

But how does one escape something such as desire? Is it really even possible? How does one transcend something that at times seems to have the power to bring us willingly, *even eagerly,* to our knees?

When I put down the phone in my hotel room in Albany, I was amazed. Whatever had happened earlier that night at Harvard Divinity School had obviously been extraordinary. According to my friend many members of the audience were reeling, awestruck. I was deeply impressed. I wasn't surprised, however. I had heard Andrew Cohen speak hundreds of times over the eight years that I had known him, and had come to expect such descriptions of his effect on people. But nothing I'd ever experienced could have prepared me for what happened when I sat down three days later to listen to a tape of this teaching, now called *The Promise of Perfection*.

Andrew's words were disarmingly simple and clear. And yet almost from the beginning they seemed to carry with them a quality, a fragrance that was like far-away music. I found myself suddenly listening in a way that is difficult to describe. As if something within me looked up startled, wide-eyed, disbelieving, and then gasped in recognition. A joy swept through me that was unbelievable to me in its depth and intensity. I felt released from prison.

The truth that is revealed here is staggering in its implications. It is shocking in its effect on one's heart. It is like being told something utterly essential to your very existence that you had once known but had long forgotten. As if before you had entered this world someone whispered in your ear *the most important thing you needed to know,* but that once here you had forgotten it.

In the small book that you now hold in your hands, Andrew Cohen has worked a miracle. In the extraordinary pages that follow, he unlocks a secret that spiritual men and women from time immemorial have suffered enormously to try to discover. There are no words to express the value of this treasure. It is a gift to all who suffer in their relationship with that seemingly almighty giant called *desire*—so it is a gift to all human beings. Do not be deceived by its size and brevity. It is that small stone, that kernel of self-knowledge that David huddled over and carefully loaded into his sling before he turned to face Goliath.

— J.B.

"One of the most difficult things in human life is to be able to see clearly, to be able to see things as they are. And after teaching continuously for many years, I can say with confidence that it is this, the ability to see clearly, that even the most sincere seekers struggle with constantly."

Illusion

Teachers of Enlightenment often use the word "illusion." They often tell us that what we are seeing is not real. This can be difficult to understand. Indeed, it can be very confusing when we are told that we're not seeing things clearly, we're not seeing things as they are, and even more, that most of what we are perceiving is actually an illusion. Needless to say, if we were to discover that this was true, that we were not seeing things as they are, it could be very intimidating, even frightening. It's the kind of thing that could scare us to death.

So from the perspective of Enlightenment, what does the word "illusion" mean? What does it mean when teachers of Enlightenment tell us that we are not seeing clearly? What does it mean when they tell us that most of the time what we are perceiving is not as it appears?

If something is illusory, it means that it literally *does not exist*. It means that what we are perceiving has no independent self-existence. It means that what we are experiencing does not exist outside of our own mind and field of sensory experience. It means, therefore, that what we are experiencing is something that we are creating with our own mind and then projecting upon the world around us.

I have found that most of us, even though we're rarely aware of it, live a great deal of our lives very much lost in and distracted by psychological and sensory experiences that have no independent reality outside the field of our own inner experience. This means that a large part of what many of us experience has no objective reality. It's something that we actually create.

Now what my own experience has taught me about this is actually quite simple, but it's also very tricky. What creates this almost perfect continuity of illusion, this unreal stream of thought and sense perception is *the endless craving, the endless wanting for personal gratification.* To some this may appear obvious, but its implications are unthinkably profound.

Wanting

To understand the implications of what it is that I'm speaking about, it is necessary to look very deeply into our own experience. You see, the experience of perfect peace, of perfect happiness, is the result of the *cessation* of the endless craving for oneself—the endless, endless wanting only for one's own self. And if we dare to look very deeply into our own experience, we find that as much as our ego hates to admit it, the truth is that those times in our lives when we have experienced the greatest happiness, which means the deepest sense of peace, are those moments when we have *ceased to want*—when for some reason or other, and it doesn't matter why, we wanted absolutely nothing from the world or from anyone in it.

Of course in the world that we live in—the world of the ego, the world of the separate personal self—equating happiness with wanting nothing doesn't make sense. In the world of the ego and personality, it is the *wanting*—the wanting of this and the wanting of that—that generates excitement, anticipation and intense longing. It's important to become aware of the fact that usually when we want something or want someone, we experience ourselves as being intensely alive, because it is then that we feel in touch with this drive within us to *have*. And this wanting, this drive to have, is experienced by the personality and ego as a positive thing. It is experienced as a very good thing. "I want for *me*. I want that for *myself*." When we think about whatever wonderful thing it is that we're interested in—a new house, a new car—it *excites* us. And it is this excitement that distorts our perception.

It's easier to get in touch with the emotional significance

of what I'm speaking about if we look into what it means to want another human being. When we strongly desire another person, who we perceive them to be in the midst of that intense longing is infinitely more than who they actually are. For example, when we fall deeply in love, we find the mere presence of the other individual intoxicating. Just to look at them is a mesmerizing experience. But interestingly enough, after we get to know them intimately, it seems impossible to sustain that same level of intoxication. We may still find them attractive, we may still feel tremendous affection for them, but that *special* something, that magic, is gone.

Now if you want a new car, if you *really* want a new car, and you decide that there is a certain car that you want to buy, then you will begin to think about that car quite a bit.

And when you see that car, you will be excited. You will love everything about it. Just looking at it will make you feel special. And when you think about the moment when you are actually going to buy that car, you will be even more excited. It's very interesting to see that, from a certain point of view, there is not that much difference between falling in love with someone and really wanting to buy a new car.

What I'm trying to bring to light is that certain objects in consciousness can often *appear* to be more than they actually are. And when certain objects in consciousness appear to be more than they actually are, it means that we are seeing *more than what is there*. We are seeing the car, we are seeing the one we long to possess, but because both are objects of our desire, we are seeing more than what's actually there. And that *more* that we are seeing *has very little to with the object itself.* It has very little to do with the car, very little to do with the attractive individual. If we look deeply enough, we will see for ourselves that in fact that *more* that we are seeing comes only from our imagination. What we are imagining is what we are *adding* to the picture. And it is what we are adding that makes our nerves dance and our heart beat a little bit faster.

You see, we may walk by that window with the new car in it every day for a year. But then one day, *bang!* Something happens. Suddenly we find ourselves seeing it differently. Now every time we stop and look at that new car, it has a profound effect on our mind and senses. It's thrilling. It's a sensual experience just to look at the car. There's an excitement in it. Before we didn't notice it, but now something has happened inside us and that particular car has become *very special*. It's the same with people. You can see a certain person every day, and then suddenly, in an instant, something can happen. It's the very same person, but now *everything* is different. Again, it's revealing to see that from a certain point of view, the experience with the car and the experience with the person are not that different.

As I said, illusion means that we are experiencing something with our mind and senses that does not actually exist, that has no independent self-existence. We are creating it. We are not seeing the car as it truly is, we are not seeing the individual as they actually are, but we are seeing the car or the individual *plus* our own imagination, our own fantasy. It's very important to understand this.

The Promise of Perfection

So when that magical something happens, when suddenly the car is not just a car but "the car *I want*," or when the individual is not just whoever they are but "the person *I want*," in that moment and in all the moments that follow, a very significant part of what it is that we're experiencing actually has nothing to do with the object itself. In fact, what we're experiencing is the power of our own desire to create the illusion of perfection. You see, when you want that car, when you really want that car but don't yet have it and can only stand in front of the window and look at it, it's not just a nice car — there's something about that car that is *magnetic*. And in that magnetism is a promise — *a promise of perfection*. And it's exactly the same kind of experience when the object of our wanting is another human being.

In the promise of perfection, when the wanting of that perfection is directed *outward* — to things, to people, to objects outside of our own selves—there is a titillation, a thrill. This thrill is a psycho-physical experience. It involves the mind and the senses. That's part of what the fun is, part of the thrill of falling in love, part of the thrill of buying that car. That's what is so exciting about it. There is literally a psycho-physical experience *in the wanting itself.* And this is why it's almost impossible for the ego and personality to recognize the experience of wanting as a bad thing—because the experience of wanting in and of itself is so thrilling. It's thrilling when you recognize a beautiful car and make the decision that you are going to have it. In that moment a light goes on inside you, and from then on, whenever you think about that car, you experience a thrill. And in that thrill there is a sense of fullness. The event of falling in love with another person who you want to have and possess, under close scrutiny, will be recognized to be an almost identical experience.

Again, it's important to understand that for the personality and ego, wanting, in the way that I'm describing it, is perceived to be a very positive experience. And it's positive because it's thrilling. Of course once we get the car and have had it for a while, it doesn't give us the same kind of thrill. As a matter of fact, only a few months after we have the new car, we may find that we now have our eye on another one. And it's exactly the same when we fall in love. After a few months, after we become familiar with the new person, it's never the same as before we were able to have them, before we were able to possess them. Now what we see is just a nice car or just a nice person. That magical something extra that made all the difference is no longer present.

You see, what is so captivating in the kind of experience that I've been describing is not the *having* of the individual or the car. Because once we are finally able to possess the object of our desire, we usually experience a process of gradual or maybe even immediate disillusionment. It's very extraordinary when we discover that the most exciting part of the whole process is the wanting itself. *It is the wanting itself that is so thrilling.* To the ego and the personality, happiness is equated with the thrill of wanting to possess, of wanting to acquire, of wanting to have *for oneself.* In this kind of wanting for oneself there is tremendous excitement. To the mind and the personality, the wanting in and of itself is perceived as an ecstatic experience.

It's very enlightening when we begin to consider the truth of our own personal experience and come to recognize that our moments of greatest joy, our moments of deepest peace and real happiness, were those when we actually *wanted nothing,* nothing at all, absolutely nothing from anyone or anything.

So if we want to be truly happy and we recognize that real happiness is found only in those times when we want absolutely nothing, then we must begin to question what our relationship to our own experience actually is.

The Challenge

To be able to see clearly, to be able to see things as they are, free from illusion and self-deception, is the goal of spiritual practice. It's not that difficult for an individual to experience some insight now and again. It's not even that unusual for a serious seeker to have an experience of transcendence — if that's what they really want. But to be able to see clearly, to be able to see things as they really are, is something else altogether. Only the individual who wants to be free more than anything else, only the individual who wants to know the truth more than anything else, will find within themselves the power of discrimination necessary to see through that which is unreal. Most of us won't be able to do it. Why? Because without knowing it, like everyone else, we will be too invested in the intensely intoxicating experience of wanting. You see, *we don't want not to want.* And this is what the problem is.

A lot of people say, "I just want to be happy, I just want to live a simple life." But it couldn't be true, because to experience real happiness, to experience true simplicity, we have to be willing to abandon the wanting. *It's only when the wanting diminishes that we can begin to experience a fullness that is always there.* That fullness is always there, and the only reason that we are not aware of it is that we are endlessly, endlessly, endlessly captivated and intoxicated by the experience of wanting.

In this world it is the experience of wanting, the intoxicating thrill of wanting, that most people are completely hypnotized by. You can be a very intelligent person and still be utterly and completely lost in the intoxication of wanting. And as long as we allow ourselves to be hypnotically distracted by that intoxication, we will never be able to see things clearly, we will never be able to see things as they really are.

There are times in life when it counts a lot more than others that we are able to see clearly — *especially those moments when we experience that wanting with the greatest intensity*. Those are the moments that count the most. Because when we want something that badly, we may be willing to do anything in order to have it. We may even be willing to deceive ourselves and others in order to be able to possess the object of our desire. The wanting can be so compelling, so thrilling that we may be unable to resist it.

This is very important to understand. It may in fact be possible for us to see clearly at times when we are very quiet and very still. But it's something else altogether when we find ourselves in the midst of the intensity of wanting. Can we, in the midst of that intensity, see through it?

Our Fundamental Relationship to Life

Seeing clearly and being able to see illusion for what it is, is entirely dependent upon our fundamental relationship to life. For most of us, our relationship to life is driven essentially by the unending desire to have and to possess. "I want for *me*" is our modus operandi. Indeed, usually this is what our fundamental relationship to all of our experience is based on. And as long as this remains the case, it will be very difficult for us to be able to see things as they are.

Now the way to be able to distinguish between truth and falsehood is not simply by trying to see clearly. Because if you're making the effort to see clearly and yet you still fundamentally want only for yourself, where are you going to end up? You're only going to be able to see with greater clarity what it is that you want for yourself.

So making the effort just to look with greater intensity is not the way that we find the ability to see clearly. If we want to be able to see clearly, we have to be willing to look into our fundamental relationship to life. When we do, we will see that almost every action that we take is motivated by this fundamental wanting for ourselves. This *"I want for me"* is expressed in gross and subtle ways thousands of times every single day—when we look, when we turn our head, when we reach out. And only when this movement slows down will we begin to notice that our perception and the way that we interpret our experience has begun to change. It changes in conjunction with the lessening of this wanting for oneself. It happens automatically.

So if we want to see clearly, it's not a matter of getting better glasses. If we want to see clearly, we have to look into our fundamental relationship to life. We have to begin to see that for most of us, our entire relationship to life is based on what is in the end a very greedy and selfish wanting only for ourselves. Merely perceiving that clearly, without any movement away from it—having the courage to experience it and to stay with it—in and of itself will open the door to another possibility, another way of being. In this other way of being we will discover, not once or twice, but over and over and over again, that real happiness, profound peace and true sanity are found only when we want *nothing*. It is then that we experience liberation from this painful wanting.

The wanting, you see, is really so painful. Of course the ego and personality experiences the wanting as pleasure. But when we look very, very closely, we become aware of the fact that the wanting is not pleasure, but pain. It's pain. It's an endless tension. And peace, joy, sanity and clarity are discovered when that tension ceases. When it ceases, and even when it only begins to lessen, instantly we feel more comfortable, more at ease. When the tension decreases even more, we feel even more at ease, more present, more at home in our own mind and body. And however unhappy a person we may have been, suddenly we find that we're comfortable being exactly who we are. This is a new experience for us, marvelous and unknown. And in this experience, the wanting and all the tension inherent in it that before we perceived as pleasure, we now recognize to be pain. This recognition has profound significance. It is the dawning of awakening.

That which makes it so difficult for us to see clearly is

the ceaseless wanting for ourselves. If we want to be able to see clearly, if we want to be able to know what's true, we have to be willing to renounce the thrill of wanting. The thrill of wanting itself is what has to be given up.

Sometimes it will be easy. At other times it will be very difficult. But it doesn't really matter. If we want to be able to see clearly, if we want to be able to see things as they are, the thrill of wanting has to be given up. And when the thrill of wanting is given up, I promise you that you will recognize that that thrill is not the pleasure it appeared to be, but is in fact pain.

So the great challenge in all of this is to find the willingness to renounce the thrill of wanting. This is the greatest challenge for the ego and the personality.

Biography

Andrew Cohen *is not just a spiritual teacher—he is an inspiring phenomenon. Since his awakening in 1986 he has only lived, breathed and spoken of one thing: the potential of total liberation from the bondage of ignorance, superstition and self-ishness. Powerless to limit his unceasing investigation, he has looked at the "jewel of enlightenment" from every angle, and given birth to a teaching that is vast and subtle, yet incomparably direct and revolutionary in its impact.*

Through his public teachings, his books and his meetings with spiritual leaders of almost every tradition, he has tirelessly sought to convey his discovery that spiritual liberation's true significance is its potential to completely transform not only the individual, but the entire way that human beings, as a race, live together. In sharp contrast to the cynicism which is so pervasive today, yet with full awareness of the difficult challenges that we face, he has dared to teach and to show that it is indeed possible to bring heaven to earth. This powerful message of unity, openness and love has inspired many who have heard it to join together to prove its reality with their own lives, igniting an ever expanding international revolution of tremendous vitality and significance.

OTHER BOOKS BY ANDREW COHEN

Freedom Has No History
Enlightenment Is a Secret
An Unconditional Relationship to Life
Autobiography of an Awakening
My Master Is My Self
Who Am I? & How Shall I Live?
An Absolute Relationship to Life
The Challenge of Enlightenment

IMPERSONAL ENLIGHTENMENT FELLOWSHIP
CENTERS FOR THE TEACHINGS OF ANDREW COHEN

Founded in 1988, Impersonal Enlightenment Fellowship is a nonprofit organization that supports and facilitates the teaching work of Andrew Cohen. It is dedicated to the enlightenment of the individual and the expression of enlightenment in the world. For more information about Andrew Cohen and his teaching, please contact:

UNITED STATES

INTERNATIONAL CENTER
P.O. Box 2360
Lenox, MA 01240
tel: 413-637-6000 or 800-376-3210
fax: 413-637-6015
email: moksha@moksha.org
website: http://www.moksha.org

NEW YORK CENTER
311 Broadway, Suite 2A
New York, NY 10007
tel: 212-233-1930
fax: 212-233-1986
email: info@faceny.org

BOSTON CENTER
2269 Massachusetts Avenue
Cambridge, MA 02140
tel: 617-492-2848
fax: 617-876-3525
email: 73214.602@compuserve.com

EUROPE

LONDON CENTER
Centre Studios
Englands Lane
London NW3 4YD UK
tel: 44-171-419-8100
fax: 44-171-419-8101
email: 100074.3662@compuserve.com
website: http://www.moksha.org/faceag.htm

AMSTERDAM CENTER
Oudeschans 46A
1011 LC Amsterdam, Holland
tel: 31-20-422-1616
fax: 31-20-422-2417
email: 100412.160@compuserve.com
website: http://www.moksha.org/face/nl

COLOGNE CENTER
Elsasstrasse 69
50677 Cologne, Germany
tel: 49-221-310-1040
fax: 49-221-331-9439
email: 100757.3605@compuserve.com

STOCKHOLM CENTER
Roslagsgatan 48nb
113 54 Stockholm, Sweden
tel: 46-8-458-9970
fax: 46-8-458-9971
email: ac.center@swipnet.se

OTHER CENTERS

SYDNEY CENTER
479 Darling Street
Balmain, Sydney
NSW 2041 Australia
tel: 61-2-9555-2932
fax: 61-2-9555-2931
email: 105312.2467@compuserve.com

RISHIKESH CENTER
PO Box 20
Sivananda Nagar, Distr. Tehri Garhwal
U.P. 249192, India
tel: 91-135-435-303
fax: 91-135-435-302
email: iefrish@nde.vsnl.net.in